PET TALK
MADE
CRYSTAL CLEAR!

What Your Pet Wants to Tell You

DAWN CRYSTAL

outskirts press

Outskirts Press, Inc.
http://www.outskirtspress.com

ISBN: 978-1-9772-2959-5

Cover Photo © 2021 John Andrick. All rights reserved - used with permission.

Outskirts Press and the "OP" logo are trademarks belonging to Outskirts Press, Inc.

PRINTED IN THE UNITED STATES OF AMERICA

DEDICATION

This is for all those who love their pets and want to understand them. It takes some guidance and an open mind to obtain the possibilities of non-traditional methods, including mine. You'll learn how I have worked with others to communicate successfully with their pets.

TABLE OF CONTENTS

FOREWORD

Dawn is a pioneer of voice-sound-energy relief of pain, anxiety, fatigue. She makes life-enhancing sounds with her voice, a gift she discovered as an adult. She has done this for over 20 years, with individuals or groups.

She has been rich and has been homeless, energetic and fatigued, and she discovered she had a gift in using her voice to relieve herself and others of troubling conditions, like pain, fear, and fatigue. This is her fifth book, all published by Outskirts Press and available online through amazon.com and bn.com, among others.

She now has a sophisticated web site, DawnCrystalHealing.com. Dawn feels a Higher Power has guided her to go Internet, go global. She started from nothing, "heart-guided."

The multitude of testimonials to the effectiveness of her technique demonstrates something beneficial is happening. We know that the mind and body are interconnected.

Those who would like to hear Dawn talk about herself and

her techniques are invited to listen to this 25-minute interview done in August 2018, https://www.talkshoe.com/conf/summary/4977560.

I have been pleased to help get Dawn's story into print as her writing coach and editor. Another kind of personal change occurred: her energy and optimism have been infectious!

Douglas Winslow Cooper, Ph.D.

douglas@tingandi.com

WriteYourBookWithMe.com

Walden, NY

Summer 2020

ACKNOWLEDGMENTS

First, and once again, I thank my coach and editor, Douglas Winslow Cooper, Ph.D., without whom this book would never have been written.

My dog, Hoku (Hawaiian for "star"), brings me daily joy and peace and deserves my gratitude. I can't imagine my life without him.

PREFACE

Many of my clients who have found relief from the sound-therapy sessions I have done with them have asked me to help their pets who have physical or "emotional" problems, and we have seen some real improvement after I worked with them.

Readers will find information herein about how our animal friends resemble us and, as our pets, support us, if we let them. You'll also find some interesting stories about animal behavior that will surprise you.

Dawn Crystal
DawnCrystalHealing@gmail.com
Maui, Hawaii
Summer 2020

PROLOGUE
WHY LIVE WITH A PET?

Even people living among friends and relatives can feel lonely, unloved, detached. Often a pet, such as a dog or a cat or a bird or even a turtle or a fish, will enhance one's life in such a situation.

First, you have an entity that needs you, relies on you, awaits you when you leave, and shows excitement when you return.

Second, you have another mind, not a human mind but still a mind, with which to interact.

Third, you have a playmate, if you wish. Whether it is "fetch" or "chase" or "come"… there are little pastimes that acknowledge each other's existence.

Finally, you are bringing pleasure to another being, and often that is given back to you.

So, I understand why you have a pet, and why I have had pets for all my adult life.

The next goal is to understand our pets, and my *PET TALK* is a step in that direction.

With love,

Dawn

Chapter 1

———✦———

How Pets Communicate

DOGS ARE PERHAPS our most familiar pets. They seem to have been made for partnership with humans, as companions and as helpers. Thousands of years of selective breeding helped bring this about, with the most suitable dogs receiving the best care and having the greatest chance of having offspring.

Dogs communicate with each other with a variety of gestures and vocalizations. Certified Professional Dog Trainer Helen A. Bemis recently published a series of books on dog-dog and dog-human communication: *Understanding Sassie; Understanding Sassie, II; Understanding Champ; Understanding Trixie, Understanding Tippie.* These are available in print or ebook through Amazon or are in press.

From her two *Sassie* books, we excerpt her vocabulary of several dog gestures:

Air snap: A dog's bite that makes no contact; dog bites the air. Excitement.

Check-in: Dog decides to come back to the person without being called.

Lip flick: Tongue quickly licks the lips. Anticipation.

Play bow: Dog leans forward with front elbows on the ground as the hips stay in the air. Invitation.

Prey bow: Back legs are tense and ready to push dog forward; elbows do not touch the ground; front legs are braced. Warning.

Besides these silent signals, we are all familiar with some common sounds dogs make: the warning bark, the welcoming bark, the asking whine, the complaining whine, the warning growl, and the excited yip.

A brief survey of books about canine communication (available at amazon. com) found these:

Canine Communications: The Language of a Species, by Sally Gutteridge;

Understanding the Silent Communication of Dogs, by Rosie Lowry;

How to Speak Dog: Mastering the Art of Dog-Human Communication, by Stanley Coren. (The Coren book had already garnered hundreds of favorable reviews.)

Decoding Your Dog: Explaining Common Dog Behaviors and How to Prevent or Change Unwanted Ones, by Debra Horwitz et al., The American College of Veterinary Behaviorists. (This book, too, had received hundreds of favorable reviews.)

Then, there is *Cesar's Way: The Natural, Everyday Guide to Understanding and Correcting Common Dog Problems,* by Cesar Milan. (This book had received over a thousand highly favorable reviews.)

Fewer books have been written about communication and cats, but here are some:

How to Talk to Your Pets: Animal Communication for Dogs, Cats, & Other Critters, by Gail Thackray

Pawstalking: A Course in Communicating with Animals, by Lisa Larson, MA

How to Speak Cat: A Guide to Decoding Cat Language, by Aline Alexander Newman and Gary Weitzman, DVM MPH

Understanding Cat Language - 50 Points, by Aude Yvanès

The Secret Language of Cats: How to Understand Your Cat for a Better, Happier Relationship, by Susanne Schötz and Peter Kuras

Among the most highly praised books in pet communication are:

Signs From Pets In The Afterlife: Identifying Messages From Pets in Heaven, by Lyn Ragan

The Cat Whisperer: Why Cats Do What They Do--and How to Get Them to Do What You Want, by Mieshelle Nagelschneider

Total Cat Mojo: The Ultimate Guide to Life with Your Cat by Jackson Galaxy

How to Get Your Cat to Do What You Want, by Warren Eckstein and Fay Eckstein

Cat Speak (Cats Rule!), by Maureen Webster

Animal Communication Made Easy: Strengthen Your Bond and Deepen Your Connection with Animals (Hay House Basics), by Pea Horsely

Horses have gotten much attention, too:

Horse Speak: An Equine-Human Translation Guide: Conversations with Horses in Their Language, by Sharon Wilsie

Zen Mind, Zen Horse: The Science and Spirituality of Working with Horses, by Allan J. Hamilton, MD; Monty Roberts, et al.

How to Think Like a Horse: The Essential Handbook for Understanding Why Horses Do What They Do, by Cherry Hill

Horses in Translation: Essential Lessons in Horse Speak: Learn to "Listen" and "Talk" in Their Language, by Sharon Wilsie

True Unity: Willing Communication Between Horse & Human, by Tom Dorrance, Milly H. Porter, et al.

Horse Psychology: An Approach to Communication at Eye Level (Ibalansi Horsemanship Book 1), by Lara-Tabitha Snyman

Horse Behaviour: Interpreting Body Language and Communication (Horse Riding and Management Series), by Barbara Schoning and Helen Grutzner

Dancing with Horses: Communication with Body Language, by Klaus Ferdinand Hempfling and Kristina McCormack

Language Signs and Calming Signals of Horses: Recognition and Application, by Rachaël Draaisma

My sound techniques engage our pets and their owners somewhat less conventionally.

During my years with cats, I noticed that if they get irritated, they start stomping the ground with their tails.

Hoku, my dog, a Pug, will bark twice to get boosted up to the couch with me. I answer, "I'll be right there." His high-pitched bark means he wants to come to bed with me or get up in it, even before I go to bed.

Hoku has it made, living in the lap of luxury. I have an SUV he snorts to signal he wants to take a ride in. To go out the front door, he scratches on it, a non-verbal communication.

My editor's dog, Colette, is a "door dog" rather than a "doorbell." She barks when people come to the door, even though the buzzer is broken. Once a delivery man came, and Colette barked, but after the man left, she kept on barking. To get her to stop, they had to go on the porch and bring in what had been delivered. Hoku behaves in much the same way, and he sounds so fierce that the delivery folk are intimidated, even though he weighs less than twenty pounds soaking wet.

I'll bet that if you pay attention to your pet, you'll find it is trying to communicate with you. Fun stuff.

Chapter 2

MY DOG IS MY MIRROR

"DOGS CAN READ Human Emotions" is the title of an article in *Reuters* by Matthew Stock in 2016. [https://www.reuters.com/article/us-dogs-emotions-idUSKCN0VP1DH]

The report is about a study in which dogs were exposed to pictures of human faces expressing various emotions and simultaneously to sounds reflecting those emotions, but in a language unfamiliar to the dogs.

"The study shows that dogs can integrate two different sources of sensory information into a perception of emotion in both humans and dogs. This means dogs must have a system of internal categorization of emotional states. Among animal groups, it's a cognitive ability previously only evidenced in primates.

"The researchers believe that the ability to combine emotional cues may be inherent to dogs. As a highly social species, detecting emotions in humans would have helped them in their domestication by people over the generations."

We already know that many people can gauge their dog's mood. In sum, dogs and people are particularly well matched for sharing emotional information about each other.

Another study, https://www.studyfinds.org/dogs-personalitychanges-owners-personalities/, found that dog personalities change as they age and are influenced by the personalities of their owners:

"Researchers at Michigan State University say dogs also have moods like humans, and their personality traits affect how they react to different situations. The study reveals that dog owners have immense influence over these traits, with such changes occurring as a response to an owner's personality or mental state. For example, people who felt happiest about their relationship with their pet tended to have a dog that was more active and excitable."

They reported that age 6 is optimal for dogs to learn new things, a bit surprising perhaps.

I have a soul connection with Hoku, my dog, whom I've had for nine years since his puppyhood. He has been a real support in my healing journey.

Sometimes, my old psychological injuries reappear. As I work on clearing myself, he seems sympathetic to my needs. Hoku, I notice, shows what is going on with me, picking up on my hurts, taking on my energy burdens.

As a child, I stored and suppressed much of my emotions, and they are surfacing from time to time. Hoku will respond by mirroring my mood.

Unfortunately, Hoku may even develop a medical problem mirroring my trauma. His unconditional love for me makes him take on my burdens, despite my asking him not to.

This dear soul-friend I take to holistic treatment when I go myself. We are treated together. His problem often cannot be fixed by a pill, just as mine cannot. Such a little dog, fifty pounds, Hoku cannot absorb all the energy overloads. His issues are on an energetic level, and he needs the kind of therapy that I give my clients.

A recent client, Ann, was a person who had been widowed twice, losing in strange car accidents two men she loved. Her youth had been very hard, as well.

Like myself, an outcast, she has had pets all her life.

In our second session, she asked me to work on her animals. She had much stored-up emotion. The dog she was closest to, Benny, a Labrador Retriever, she would hear at night breathing very heavily at the foot of her bed, as though he were dealing with a heavy load. Her vet diagnosed Benny as having excessive stress on his organs.

I could tell that Ann had retained much-blocked energy, and it was important to clear her first, which we did. She was very anxious, and we worked on releasing the stored emotions that were affecting her adrenal glands.

"Now, let us work on Benny," I told her. I could tell that his adrenals were also stressed, just as Ann's were. "Benny, is it OK if I work on you?" I always ask the pets for permission. His response, telepathically, indicated he wanted me to do this.

I moved Benny's energy through his adrenals and kidneys, and I could tell he needed help. Ann indicated he began yawning and stretching, good signs, within a few minutes of my activities.

I asked, "How's Benny looking now?" Animals respond with different speeds from humans. "This is Benny's mission: to support you. As you get better, so will he. You might reassure him that you are feeling better."

Both of them seemed better, and Ann thanked me. I'll be checking with her on our next session.

We should always let our animals know that we are working on our issues, and reassure them that we are getting better, which they will also sense on an energy level.

Chapter 3

---✦---

A Dog With A
Puzzling Problem

HOKU, MY 9-YEAR-OLD fur baby, is the love of my life. He has sensed my going through many physical changes as I relived and coped with the anxieties from my childhood.

Hoku would pick up on my tensions. As I worked on myself, I would see him responding beneficially. My soul-dog empathized with me, and being less than 50 pounds, his energy would change rapidly.

For example, constipation became a surprising problem with him for a period. It is rare in animals. I would even have to give him saline enemas. Something was going on. It turned out he was mirroring my frustration. Now that I have cleared these problems in my own life, he is doing better as well.

Yesterday I worked with Patricia, who has worked with me in the past. She got one of my telesummit programs. She had body pain issues for many years that needed helping. So impressed with our sessions, she bought another program of mine that included a session with me intended to help her dog.

This was a 25-minute session. Her dog, Skippy, is a mid-size dog with a puzzling problem causing fevers, fatigue, and some other issues. They live in New York State, and the dog was bitten by a tick, which could be one cause, perhaps Lyme disease. We decided Skippy should stay on antibiotics.

Some of the dog's problems started before the tick bite. The dog has been crucial to her, as her husband has passed away. She lives in Manhattan, and the rising costs of living there are pushing her out, making her move. So, she's downsizing, getting ready to find a more manageable place, feeling very stressed in getting ready to move without help. She'd hire a handyman, but they are hard to get and too expensive.

I figured that the dog is picking up on her stress. We worked on Patricia first, to help Skippy also. It became clear that Patricia's energy was affecting her pet.

I offered her some down-to-earth advice, "You need to check out less expensive help, like through Craigslist."

"Yes, that makes sense"

Her energy was stagnated. As I worked on this, I could tell that Skippy, in the room with her, felt Patricia's tension lessening.

"You mean my dog has been taking in my stress?"

"Yes, and his body is too small to take on such an overload of negative energy."

I worked on her...to help her dog, as she understood. We worked on clearing her blocked energy passages. She felt better.

She brought Skippy closer to the phone. He was biting his paws, from nervousness. As I made my sounds, he relaxed. We cleared Skippy easily. This small dog responded rapidly.

"What's he doing?" I asked.

"He's yawning and stretching. He seems much more relaxed."

"Good. Reassure him that you are feeling better and that you will be able to handle what is coming up."

Chapter 4

CASPER, A DOG THAT SERVED,
THEN SUFFERED

THERE ARE GUIDELINES established for what legally constitutes a "service dog" and what constitutes an "emotional support dog," and a link provided by the American Kennel Club is a good start:

https://www.akc.org/expert-advice/lifestyle/
everything-about-emotional-support-animals/

The dog, Casper, I will tell you about next is not officially in either of these two categories, but like so many pets, he serves, nonetheless.

Before I tell you his story, I'll note that I searched the Internet for articles on whether or not emotional support dogs themselves suffer from stress. The most appropriate article did not quite answer that question, but did list five signs your dog is stressed:

1. Diarrhea, Constipation, or other Digestive Issue
2. Decrease in Appetite
3. Isolation
4. Increased Sleeping
5. Aggression Toward People or Other Animals

If you observe these for a prolonged period, you should consult your veterinarian.

One of the people who bought my programs, Sally, had bought my "Get out of Pain Forever." Soon after, we talked on the phone about pain.

"Hi, Sally. How can I help you?"

"I was impressed by your telesummit talk. I'm on my feet a lot, as a nurse, loving my work, but working long hours at a demanding job. My legs hurt and I'm stressed."

"I understand. I can tell you also have tension in your neck and shoulders. Besides, you have a blockage in your legs, making you feel heavy."

"Yes, Dawn, this has been a continuing problem for me."

"I'll get your energy moving through your body, breaking up areas of stagnation. Anything else going on?"

"I do some volunteer work. I have two Labrador Retrievers, whom I bring with me to nursing homes to comfort the residents. My Labs like to go with me to visit these people. One of the dogs, Casper, is showing some problems at seven years of age. He comes with me every couple of weeks to the nursing homes. This mission of ours brings happiness to the residents, and we have done it for four years so far. A lot of people at home know me. When we come back, Casper seems bushed and for days doesn't act like himself. He's lethargic."

"We'll work on you first. Relax. View a divine light above your head. Sit in a safe place, as you may get an energy rush from my work with you."

"OK, I'll stay seated."

I made my sounds and had her picture energy leaving her body. I could see in my mind energy leaving her body, past the blockages, especially past the feet and legs, then the calves, and up through her body. "Are your knees hurting?"

"They have been."

We did more energy movement with my sounds, rapid energy movement. It seemed to be working. We went through her kidney area, to get them working properly.

"Have you had a major trauma in your life?" Turned out her parents divorced when she was young, leading to a lot of stress.

While with me on the phone, she cried a bit, releasing sadness from her childhood. We then cleared her various chakras. "How are you feeling now?"

"Oh, my gosh! You are a miracle healer! I've worked with others and not had anything as wonderful as this. I have been blessed!"

"Very good, Sally, I see we have made real progress. Let's see what we can do for Casper."

It was clear to me that Casper, like Hoku my dog, is an "old soul." He likes going to nursing homes and bringing them hope. He likes to cheer them up and likes their petting him. As did Hoku, he was taking on the harmful energy loads of these patients and bringing the energy home with him.

I spoke directly to him, "Casper, it is fine to help the people at these homes, but you must not bring their problems home with you, or you will need to go to the vet for medical treatment." I felt he was understanding me. I made some energy sounds for him. He is doing charitable work and deserves not to suffer. I cleared the excess, stagnated energy.

"Sally, what is Casper doing now?"

"Stretching and yawning."

"That's just what he should be doing. Be aware when you go into the nursing homes that you need to put a white light shield mentally around you and Casper at these homes, to protect your-selves, so you can go home feeling good, without carrying a load from the patients there,"

"That makes sense. Casper wants to help, sometimes more than he can handle. I'll let you know how things go."

A month or so later, she reported that Casper and she were doing better now that she has put an energy boundary around the two of them on their way to the nursing home.

She thanked me again, "Your session was a life-changing event for both of us."

I love this story. We have to be aware that we have an energy side to us as well as a physical one. We must maintain our true selves by being aware of and not taking on everyone else's problems. Our pets have energy systems that need protection, too. You can do what brings you joy. Just imagine that protective boundary around you and your pets as you go about your day.

Chapter 5

───── ❧ ─────

CATS HAVE PROBLEMS, TOO, SUCH AS PROPHETIC POOPING

WHAT IS YOUR cat telling you? An excellent book on the topic is *Understanding Cat Language - 50 Points,* by Aude Yvanès. Here are some of the 50 sounds and gestures described (with drawings) in this delightful book:

- Aggression; ears back, mouth open, growl: back off!

- Attacking you while being stroked: doesn't want this now.

- Attacking your shoes: time to play. Gently rap his nose if you want to discourage this.

- Fear: ears back and body curled.

- Growling: discontented, even afraid. May spit and attack.

- Happiness: eyes half-closed, ears forward.

- Meow, meow, meow: something is wrong. Needs help.

- On guard: hides, tense, slinks, eyes possible prey.

- Purring: usually signifies pleasure.

- Respectful offering: a small dead animal on your doorstep.

- Serenity: resting on the side, ears slightly erect. All is well.

- Squealing: pain. Needs help.

I have an affectionate connection with animals, who have sometimes made better friends than many humans in my life.

When I was sixteen, I lived in a garage apartment; a neighbor took me in. I was working as a hostess and had enough money to care for two cats, at least for a while. The cats from the animal shelter were Spoon and Fork, brother and sister.

In the garage apartment, I had no other companion, no other love, but these cats were adorable, affectionate, and entertaining as they played with each other. Great experience, much better than my childhood hamsters! They were my buddies. I fostered them and found them homes after a few months. I must say they added a lot to my life. They were very loving. I wished I could have kept them.

A client, Brenda, bought a telesummit session on another topic. Before the session, she noted she also wanted some help with her cat, Fluffy. I was fine with that.

"Hi, Brenda. Thanks for getting my program. You noted your cat had some behavior problems you wanted help with."

"I've had my problems. My husband, my soul partner, died after only five years of our marriage. Healing has been slow.

"Finally, I joined a dating site. Still in my forties, I have put myself out there to do some dating. I've had a few good dates and some bad. My cat is loving with me, but standoffish with others who visit."

"Yes, animals have their own personalities."

"A year ago, Fluffy was so reserved with one of my dates to the point that it puzzled me. That match did not work out. Also, I've noticed that since my husband died and I have started dating, Fluffy has been pooping in parts of the house and hiding it, not using his litter box. Something is awry. Can you tune into Fluffy? I hope you can help him. This is very awkward"

Brenda brought Fluffy close to the phone. I wanted to clear Brenda to start.

"Let's clear you first. How are you?"

"Since the death of my husband, I have often been very sad. I feel him near me at times. We did not have enough time to say goodbye to each other."

"Shall we work on that?" Yes, she wanted to. "You are holding some emotions you need to clear."

"I do think he wants me to date others now." I made some sounds and released energy from Brenda's stomach past her heart and then to her head and out to a light above her head. She started to cry.

"How are you feeling?" I asked.

"I feel my trapped emotions being released, and my heart seems to be expanding."

My clearing sounds continued. "How are you now?"

"Much better."

I said, "Let's work with Fluffy." He turned out to be mirroring her emotions. "He is letting you know that he is aware of the energies of the people you are dating. His pooping indicates he does not like the energy of the person you brought in."

"Are you kidding? Really? He is telling me which of these people seems good for me? I have not been all that successful, as people on the dating site have generally not been what they presented themselves to be; for example, they have pictures on the dating site of them when they were ten years younger."

"Pay some attention to what Fluffy is telling you. This dating process is not working out well. His pooping can be taken as a clue."

"I'll pay attention to that."

Fluffy was by the phone, and I made my sounds. Brenda reported that he stretched and looked a lot more relaxed.

I look forward to hearing more from her.

In general, I feel that animals do try to connect with us, even though they cannot speak. We have to pay attention to the signals they give us. Fluffy loved Brenda and wanted her to have a good person in her life, not one who might cause her problems.

Chapter 6

———∾———

CAT'S PEE PROBLEM
SENDS A MESSAGE

WE ARE USED to the idea that dogs are smart, but recent work has shown that cats are, too, and that they can communicate with us successfully. A fine article in *Scientific American* in 2016 highlighted the abilities of cats and humans to communicate with each other. [https://blogs.scientificamerican.com/not-bad-science/what-we-understand-about-cats-and-what-they-under-stand-about-us/]

The article's author, Felicity Muth, writes, "Since cats have both been bred to be domestic and spend a lot of time with humans, we would expect them to pick up on human cues to some extent. However, anyone who has owned a cat knows that they are not always as responsive as you might want them to be."

Researchers, Muth notes, found that cats could be directed to objects by having humans point at them, although cats did not seek human guidance when searching for lost items. Another study found that cats were more or less scared of an unfamiliar object depending on how nearby humans were reacting. Cats are less likely to approach humans who are feeling depressed. Cats responded to their owners' voices more than to the voices of strangers.

Muth cited another study, concerning vocalization: *Kittens have around 9 different types of vocalization, while adults have around 16 different types. Interestingly, domestic and feral cats also differ from each other in their vocalizations, implying that their relationships with humans influence how cats 'talk'. Perhaps one of the most renowned vocalizations of cats is their purr. Cats don't just purr when being stroked by humans, they also use it in interactions with each other and with their kittens. What's more, cats alter their purr to change the meaning of the vocalization.*

Cats put into an empty room or one having a stranger or one having their owner, behave differently, in each case. Furthermore, they respond to undesirable situations in various ways, as Muth summarizes, "When separated from their human owners, **cats are more likely to display stress behaviors such as urinating and defecating in inappropriate locations**, excessive vocalization, destructiveness, and excessive grooming." (Our emphasis added.)

Growing up, in my teens, we had a cat. Fluffy was very smart, and I found him interesting.

Actually, he was Mom's cat. To let the family know what was on his little feline mind, he would pee in the bathtub when displeased. During one period, feeling unnoticed, he kept doing this until they noted blood in his urine. A trip to the vet cured his urinary tract problem, if not his attitude.

A year or so ago, I worked with a woman, Melody, who lived on the East Coast of the USA. She found me through my program about opening the heart, healing the heart, my "The Discover Sound Healing Program."

She had a session with me.

"How can I serve you?"

"I was moved by your story about your childhood and failed marriages. I work to keep myself attractive, and I'm in my mid-50s, but I just cannot find love. I attract the wrong guys, misfits, men with baggage. Fortunately, I love animals, and they provide the love that I am not getting in my romances. I have four cats, originally strays. I was never married and have no children, so these are my 'fur babies.'

"On the dating sites, the men put pictures that are not realistic: in person, they are ten years older and at least ten pounds heavier. My cats sense this lack of attraction. One cat, Billy the Kid, has responded to several of these visitors. He tends to hide when they come and pee in the corner."

"Let's talk about you, Melody. I sense you have a closed heart, that you do not love yourself. Have you had some trauma?"

"One of my babysitters molested me when I was four, and I have been uncomfortable with sexual interaction ever since. Now, at 55, I'd like to be able to have regular relationships and find a mate. At these dating sites, I have met men and brought some home. When I wanted to introduce the new men to my animals, Billy would hide out and sometimes even pee in the corner, not in the litter box. I would smell it later, and I finally figured it out. The vet checked on

Billy, and there was not any urinary problem. I don't know what is going on. Could you clear me first, then work on my cat?"

"Sure." She did have signs of childhood trauma that had closed her heart chakra and upset her stomach chakra. I also sensed constipation problems, and she worked with me as I moved her energy, releasing blocked energy through the top of her head.

She started crying deeply. Several times I stopped briefly to check to see if she felt OK.

She responded that she was "happy" to be crying, "I can feel my heart opening. Oh, my gosh, I feel more alive, better than I have ever felt, ecstatic…. Can you also help my cat?"

I asked Billy the Kid what was going on. The cat responded that he does not like some of these people and to communicate this he pees in the corner. He has objected to the negative energy they left behind.

I cleared Billy rapidly. Melody noted he was stretching and yawning during the treatment.

Melody said that she felt Billy and she were soul-connected. She understood that he was doing this out of love.

I recommended that Melody be more selective about whom she invites home and that she clear the house atmosphere with incense, such as sage or frankincense.

"I think in the future I will first invite these new people to meet with me first at a coffee shop, and only bring home the ones I really trust."

Subsequently, she told me that selecting the guests this way and our having Billy the Kid cleared had put an end to his persistent pissing problem.

Chapter 7

———✦———

A Horse Too Easily Spooked

Horses have been "spoken to" for years by humans. One highly successful trainer was called "the horse whisperer."

Trainer Sharon Wilsie has written a highly acclaimed book on the topic, *Horse Speak: An Equine-Human Translation Guide: Conversations with Horses in Their Own Language.* This is available at amazon.com at

https://www.amazon.com/Horse-Speak-Equine-Human-Translation-Conversations-ebook/dp/B0733B26FL/ref=sr_1_1?keywords=communicating+with+horses&qid=1565893583&s=books&sr=1-1

My search on "communicating with horses" had yielded 87 books at amazon.com. For conventional methods of horse-human dialogue, one can get plenty of good advice.

I never owned a horse. I did ride one once. My foolish drinker of a father took us out for riding one time during a so-called "vacation," and I returned so bruised up afterward from horseback riding at a roadside riding "academy" on an untrained brute, I could hardly sit for a week. It was like a wild bull ride in a rodeo. What a vacation for a nine-year-old!

Of course, I have my own methods of "communicating," and my sounds proved of value for someone I know well: a friend, "Jane," here on Maui, is a teacher's aide and a horse trainer. We were chatting one evening. She had a client at a horse farm with several horses she was asked to train. They were not calm, almost wild. Something was upsetting them. They seemed "spooked." She knows I do psychological sound-healing work with humans, and she hoped I could help them.

"How long has this been going on?" I asked Jane.

"Ever since they moved to a new location six months ago. Something about this new place has them upset. They are forgetting their training. They are supposed to be calm on the trail rides, but instead are easily upset, spooked. Can you help?"

"I'll give it a try."

I went there to help. The property struck me as having an unsettling energy level. I have cleared land and homes of bad vibrations before. It has even helped sell a home more rapidly. This treatment is a little like some Chinese do in their homes using *Feng Shui*.

Certain areas in Hawaii have been the sites of battles in the past, and the animals can pick up those energy vibrations. I used my voice to start clearing the property. It took me about a half-hour.

Then I worked with the five horses. Three of the five were nervous. All five seemed to respond well to my clearing. Some needed grounding. Taking them from one environment to another had been upsetting. This grounding process took me an additional half-hour. I told the owner to give the horses a few days to get used to the new situation. He agreed. The owner himself had felt unsettled when walking his land at night.

A few weeks later, they told me my clearing had helped the horses and the owner to feel more at ease. Their being spooked was cured. Now they could use all five horses for the trail rides, and that has helped their revenue situation.

Chapter 8

———— ✤ ————

"Bird Brain" Is A Compliment!

Birds are markedly different from us, and yet it turns out they are surprisingly smart. A search on "intelligence of birds" on Amazon produced a wealth of books displaying avian intelligence rivaling that of mammals such as dogs and chimps and even humans. Here are five:

- *The Genius of Birds,* by Jennifer Ackerman

- *Bird Brains: The Intelligence of Crows, Ravens, Magpies, and Jays,* by Candace Savage

- *Bird Brain: An Exploration of Avian Intelligence,* by Nathan Emery and Frans de Waal

- *Secret Life of Birds: Who They Are and What They Do,* by Colin Tudge

- *Alex & Me: How a Scientist and a Parrot Discovered a*

Hidden World of Animal Intelligence--and Formed a Deep Bond in the Process, by Irene Pepperberg

Ackerman's *The Genius of Birds* describes the extraordinary abilities of various bird species from all over the world: birds making tools, solving puzzles, knowing "fifth" from "second," being adept at learning tricks and language, members of a class of animals here on Earth for over 100 million years, present all over the globe, outnumbering humans by about 50 to 1, indicating exceptional survival capability, an important skill. She notes: *There's a species that solves a puzzle at nearly the same pace as a five-year-old child, and one that is an expert at picking locks. There are birds that can do simple math, make their own tools, move to the beat of the music, comprehend basic principles of physics, remember the past and plan for the future.*

Pepperberg's *Alex & Me* deals with the personal relationship she developed with a brilliant parrot, a member of a species widely known for its intelligence. Those who have parrots or parakeets are familiar with how smart they seem to be, and Pepperberg's Alex was convincing in his abilities and touching in his sentiments.

It won't surprise you that a few of my clients have come to me with issues that related to their pet birds.

Chapter 9

An Emotional Support Pony Tale, Not A Ponytail

In September of 2019, a miniature pony emotional support animal became somewhat famous, as it was allowed to take an airplane trip with its owner, as reported in the *UK Metro News* by reporter Elisa Menendez:

> *Passengers on a recent American Airlines flight to Omaha, Nebraska, were shocked to find themselves sharing the aisle with a miniature pony. The service animal, called Flirty, was seen boarding the flight from Chicago, Illinois, with its owner last week. And it wasn't long before passengers began sharing videos of tiny Flirty casually pottering through the airport on a lead. Another clip shows Flirty having a snooze with its owner onboard the flight.*
>
> *[Read more: https://metro.co.uk/2019/09/02/woman-pictured-sitting-service-horse-plane-10670918/?ito=cbshare]*

While there are rules and regulations governing service animals and emotional support animals, we are likely to see more of these helpful pals, rather than fewer. What follows is a story from my own experience.

I worked with "Emily" recently about an issue concerning her and her emotional support pet, a miniature pony.

This began after I started helping Emily's daughter, Kris, a Californian. We've done a couple of years together after she found me on a telesummit. Kris has a farm in California. Her major issue is not knowing how to save money. She and her husband, who is not much of a worker, have several horses and three children. Kris trains horses, and she farms, too.

Kris and I worked on stress relief for her. A warm, empathetic person, she loves her lazy husband, a sports fanatic. She goes to work, returns home, often finds he has not fed the animals. There must have been a Big Game on TV!

In our second session, after doing some preliminary stress relief, we talked about money. She is living month to month, going nearly broke, yet still wants to have the farm and the animals. We worked on reducing stress and manifesting abundance.

The third session was for Kris's mom, Emily, who has a problem with being very nervous. Emily is in her 80s and is still quite active. Emily has bonded with one of the baby miniature ponies, which has comforted her better than a dog or a cat. Emily recently lost her husband. The baby pony, Robbie, really consoled her. Unfortunately, she wasn't supposed to take the pony everywhere, as some places don't want her to come with the animal. When Robbie is rejected, Emily gets upset.

Kris told her the pony is an impractical pet for going out to other places, but her mother did not want to stop.

Emily was open to working with me. I thought I could help her with her emotional needs, and I could reassure her that some of these trips could be done alone.

On the phone, I started with, "Hi, Emily, your daughter has treated you to this package out of love for you. Tell me about yourself."

"I was in a big family, and our parents were nice, but they had little time for each of us, leaving me lonely. I was pretty much ignored, and I did not fit in at school. I came to love the horses and ponies on our farm."

"Emily, many of us have a liking for certain animals, but you need to feel ok when you cannot have your pet with you. Not all establishments are comfortable with having a pony there. First, though, let's clear your energy blockages and relieve your stress."

I made some of my sounds and told her that we were going to remove her feeling of being unworthy.

She acknowledged, "The only time I have felt safe has been on the farm with the ponies."

"We'll work on this fear and clear the trauma." I made some more of my special sounds.

Suddenly, she told me her body had started shaking. Via the telephone, she was responding to my sounds. We did some grounding, as she lacked this from her childhood. We rid her of her fight-or-flight response. It only took one session.

"How are you doing now?" I asked her.

"Much better. I'm relaxed, even yawning, as though I were with my baby pony or if I had taken my melatonin pills. I am very relaxed."

I made more sounds and had her breathe deeply. "How are you now?"

"I feel you are very competent. I am stable in my body, a feeling I've never had before. I feel I now am ok."

"See if you can sometimes leave Robbie behind when you go out and have both of you get used to it."

She said she would do that and would ask her daughter Kris to tell me how it worked out.

Kris told me later that her mother did change and only takes the pony to the places where it is welcome. She is not as desperate for it to be with her. The transformation is clear. She joined a seniors' club, where they play some board games, and she has made some friends there. She is less dependent on her sweet pet pony and is probably more widely welcomed.

Some other clients have had emotional support animals and some others thought they would benefit from having them. Even better, those needing such support could benefit from one of our sound sessions, to make them feel OK without having something outside themselves to cling to. I help them to understand they are already whole, and much that people choose to add to their lives are mere additions, not necessities.

Chapter 10

———◆———

TALE OF A TURTLE TAIL

FOR MONTHS WHEN I would come home to the apartment, one I had already lived in for ten years, I had something strange happen. Let me explain.

I had a dog, Hoku, and I fed twice a day two cats that freely roamed the neighborhood. Sometimes you don't "own" cats, you only "rent" them.

Then, the landlord moved in next door, along with a half-dozen parrots, nine cats, and three dogs. The place went from tranquil to chaotic: animal sounds constantly.

I would leave for work most mornings, and I would leave the door ajar for my dog to go in and out. My dog was about seven. Hoku and I were old pals, and he knew what to do on his own, doing his business by "going to the bathroom" outside while I was gone.

One day when I came home, I smelled some poo. Where did that come from? I looked around and found a big mound under my bed, an impressive mound, bigger than what Hoku would produce. What was up with that?

Is Hoku OK? Is this from the cats?

Hoku was well, and the cat poop was different from this.

Two weeks later, I found my TV crashed on the floor, a trail of slime through my home, and a mound of crap under my bed.

I asked the landlord, David, but he did not know what was happening.

"I know my dog is not doing this. Could this be due to yours, David?"

"No, they are chained up the yard. Could something else be coming in through your door?"

The problem recurred a couple of weeks later: cat food eaten, TV knocked down, slime on the floor, and a mountain of *merde* under the bed.

"Hoku, is this you?" I asked my innocent dog.

Hoku told me it was done by a turtle, coming in to eat the cat food.

The next day, I did not go to work. I saw this huge land turtle in my house!

I contacted my landlord. "David, is this your turtle?"

"No, not ours."

We found that it came from a next-door neighbor's yard, having dug a big hole under the fence between us. The turtle preferred our cat chow to their turtle cuisine. It came right through door and into our home.

We told those neighbors. Turned out that this massive reptile was called "Dozer," as in "bulldozer."

Its "master" admitted, "Yeah, Dozer tends to wander around."

"Well, he broke my table and made a mess in my house, and this needs to stop!"

Soon after, the titanic turtle found another way into the house. This time, Dozer would not leave my home, and he slept the whole day under my bed. We finally got him back to the neighbors. They offered to fix the fence and gave the turtle away.

So, Hoku, my sweet pooch, was not only innocent, but he solved the messy Maui mystery and identified the reptilian culprit. The poop problem got resolved.

We don't know what happened to Dozer, the mighty pooper, probably making mammoth *merde* mounds elsewhere in Maui, but fortunately for me not in my home.

Bad times make good stories.

Chapter 11

———❦———

THE DISAPPEARING CAT

THIS CLIENT OF mine was Mary, owner of a smiling cat that disappeared, like the Cheshire cat in *Alice in Wonderland*.

She called the cat "Happy," though it wasn't always happy.

Mary had found me from a telesummit, about a year before. Her problems had nothing to do with her cat, except that her feline friend did come up late in the session.

This is a New York City woman, secretary to a lawyer or lawyers. High-pressure job. "Unlimited Energy" was my program she bought.

"Thanks, Mary, for purchasing the program."

"I really resonated with you when I heard you on the telesummit. I knew you could help me. I'm glad to have a private session."

"What's happening?"

"I'm an executive secretary at a high-pressure law firm here in the City. For the last few years, I'm finding myself slowing down, getting drained. There are also issues in my private life."

"Are you single? Engaged?"

"Just broke up with a guy who was cheating on me. Also, the love of my life – my cat, Happy – started disappearing on me. She was a rescued cat, from the pound. I adopted her when I noticed she had a little smile on her puss at the shelter. A snow-white cat, I fell in love with her. She often wanted to go outside and explore, but I was reluctant to do it until I saw that others were letting their cats out. Happy would go out and about outside, without problems, and the neighbors found her to be friendly. Then she disappeared for a whole week. I was really worried. She finally came back. Actually, even while gone, she came back daily to eat the food I left for her at the door, but she did not come in to be with me. I asked myself, 'Does she not want to be with me anymore?' I felt I'd lost connection with her."

"What happened then?"

"Happy disappeared again one night, and I decided to follow her. I let her out, then walked behind her. Happy went down the street, about a block away, went through a yard, and then she went into a pile of boxes. Happy was mothering kittens that were not hers! She was a foster mother, having been neutered. She couldn't nurse them, but she was keeping the kittens warm. Recently, she brought all five kittens home, and she is here now, and my house is full of cats. Happy is home, but so are the five furry foster kittens. I'm not sure what to do."

"Really cool story, Mary."

"Dawn, I need some peace for myself. Help!"

I cleared Mary of her scattered energy, and I centered her. We cleared a lot of chaotic energy. She is an empath but has trouble handling all the energy that she absorbs from other people. I grounded her life-force energy, through her feet.

"How are you now?"

"So much better, Dawn; my head feels clearer."

"Exactly."

I helped her with the heartbreak of her fiancé's cheating on her.

"Oh, good, I've been suffering from my work and the cats, but I needed to get over the break-up, too."

I moved the heart pain energy from that chakra. She was holding in a lot of emotional energy about someone she had loved.

I had Mary ask her cat what Happy wanted to do. We found that Happy wanted feline companionship, and so Mary decided to keep a kitten or two to keep Happy happier.

I ended the session with a final integrating sound. I had Mary take a deep breath, and then I asked her, "How do you feel now?" "I fell so much better, and I can finally think straight. I can tell that Happy is going to be more content in the new situation."

I have not heard from Mary, but I believe she and Happy are happier and so are an adopted kitten or two...or three.

I find it very sweet that animals have the generous impulse to mother another's babies, just as many a woman would do in a similar situation. So much love!

Since then, we found a somewhat similar story from April 2018. Jake Levin of NBC 10 Boston, reported, "Cat Hailed as Hero for Nursing Another Cat's Kittens."

"A mother cat, Church, was unable to give her kittens enough milk, and they were in grave danger.

"Enter Betty: a 2-year-old orange tab cat had been dropped off at the shelter prior to Church's arrival, after she was abandoned in an apartment building. It just so happened that Betty was lactating, despite not having any kittens of her own. Alyssa Krieger, the community outreach coordinator at the MSPCA, introduced Church's kittens to Betty in hopes that she would nurse them back to health."

You can guess the rest: Betty let the kittens nurse and eventually Church did, too, and the whole crew ended up doing very well.

[https://www.nbcboston.com/news/local/Cat-Hailed-As-Hero-for-Nursing-Another-Cats-Kittens-478784173.html]

Given that Mary's Happy was not lactating, it is perhaps even more unusual that she took to caring for this little brood of foster-kittens.

Chapter 12

———∿∿∿———

ANN'S SON NEEDED PETS IN THE BED

IS IT SAFE for you or your child to have a dog sleep in the bed with you? Nancy Dunham wrote an article about this for petmd.com, from which I'll quote:

Go ahead and sleep with your dog—it's perfectly safe, as long as you are both healthy.

In fact, sharing your bedroom with your canine companion— as long as he isn't under the covers—may actually improve your sleep, according to recent research published by <u>Mayo Clinic Proceedings.</u> Although researchers didn't study the impact of felines sleeping with their pet parents, anecdotally, veterinarians suggest the results are mostly positive (though the nocturnal cat may be a bit more disruptive)....

Like adult pet parents, young children often want to sleep with the family dog or cat. All cases differ, of course, but it's generally unwise to have a child of 6 or younger sleep alone with a pet.

~~~

A similar issue arose in a session I had with one of my clients. Her child, Tommie, was about five years old and nearly deaf. He had lost much of his hearing at six months old, and that may have contributed to his anxiety.

His mom, "Ann," discovered me from a friend of a friend who had found me on a telesummit. Ann hoped I could help her with stress and emotional issues, such as depression. She had purchased one of my programs.

"Hi, Ann, you are new to my work. I understand that you've tried almost everything, and you are worried about your child, Tommie. Thanks for purchasing my program. Let's make it as enjoyable and profitable for you as we can."

"I've been searching for help, Dawn. I'd like you to split this session, help me with part of the session, then help my son."

"Fine." I do that sometimes.

"I'm on the East Coast, 55 years old, married for many years; my husband and I knew each other as teens. He is having problems with drinking. I'm staying in the marriage for the kids primarily. My son is nearly deaf, and I have to handle this situation. My husband is having trouble coping with his son's deafness and with his drinking, which sometimes enrages him.

"Thanks for splitting the session up. I'm a nervous wreck, and I have financial issues. My daughter, when four, was left with Tommie, and she may have been jealous. I should have kept an eye on her. She screamed at him for so long and so loud that he lost much of his hearing, and the hospital could not fix it.

"Tommie is now five and still can barely hear nor speak. Kids are teasing him about this. We are trying to keep him in regular school. He likes pets a lot. He needs them to be around him. We've adopted three dogs and two cats, many of which like to share the bed with him. He has bad allergies, and we want to let him keep the pets even though they may aggravate the allergies. Can you help Tommie with his anxiety? Look at his energy. He can hear you somewhat with his hearing aid."

I made some sounds for Ann, first. She needed help and was affecting Tommie with her concern. "Put a beautiful, divine light above your head, and now imagine your toxic energy leaving you and going into that light. We are going to ground your life-force energy. This will help you think clearly and be calmer, which will help him."

I made my sounds for a few minutes. We had worked for half the session.

"These are the most peaceful, angelic sounds I've ever heard, and I feel much calmer. I even feel my legs as I have not felt them before. Let's work with Tommie. With his pets in his bed, he has hardly room to sleep."

I talked with Tommie and made some sounds. I had him imagine a white light above his head, and I made some of my sounds.

"Breathe calmly, Tommie. Let your heavy thoughts go into God's light."

"I know Mom does not want me to have the pets sleep with me."

It took a bit longer than usual to get started with him. A five-year-old child, he knew I wanted to help him.

"Let all of this go. You have gone through a lot, but it can be changed."

"I forgive my sister." That was a surprising statement, a very generous one.

Yes, Tommie did have congested energy in his ears, among other locations. I drained the excess energy through his feet to the ground.

"How are you starting to feel? Any popping in your ears?"

"Yes, they feel like a bubble opened. I can feel it. Feels good. I feel more relaxed."

A pretty amazing child, he understood more than I would have expected. He told me that when he went to adopt animals at the shelter, the ones he chose told him they wanted him to take them home and that if he did not bring them home, they would be killed.

"Wow! Tommie, I can talk with the animals, too. The animals are helping you with getting along with the kids at school. They make it easier for you."

PET TALK MADE CRYSTAL CLEAR!

"Right."

"Maybe you can tell them they should help you by sleeping on the floor rather than on the bed. Mom, how is he looking, now?"

"Much more alert, awake, rather different from usual. This may help him pay attention in school."

"He talks to his pets, Ann, and he knows which ones want to come home with him."

"Yes, Dawn, he does seem to have a gift for that."

"He might do well to ask some of them to sleep on the floor instead of on the bed. The animals are helping him, making it easier for him to interact with other kids."

"Wow, Dawn! That's cool."

I asked her to let me know how he makes out. She thanked me for clarifying his situation and assuring her that Tommie could indeed converse with his pets.

"I understand your son, because I had that same ability all my life, communicating with animals."

"Thank you, Dawn."

About three months later, she contacted me, and she took another session with me. She told me that Tommie was doing much better, which she attributed to the work we did on the phone. She and he both felt better. She is thinking about having her husband get a session, also.

I find that a lot of children are opening up to different abilities not understood before. As a five-year-old, I had these abilities, but they were not believed by adults, and I had to hide them. In cases like Tommie's, I let both child and parent know that a special ability is there, one that may let the child, as an adult, improve the planet!

People should be open to the possibility that their children have such special skills. Ann was open, and she received a very positive surprise.

Chapter 13

———— ᴥ ————

CHAMP, A REAL CHAMPION

ALICE IS A listener to our telesummits. She owns a farm in Minnesota, and she has a herding dog, perhaps a Border Collie. She asked me to work with her and then with her dog.

Alice's problem was that her hair was falling out, due to anxiety. She was in her early sixties, worried about going bald prematurely; it bothered her a lot because she had long been proud of her hair.

"How long has this hair loss been going on?" I asked Alice.

"Off and on throughout my life. As a child, I was abused by an alcoholic father. Now, I raise goats and chickens, with help from my dog, Champ."

Before she told me this, I had told her that I noted trauma in her energy, something we could ground with sound. I cleared her energy into the light. Fortunately, she was open to my work.

Drugs had not helped with her fear nor with her hair loss. With my sounds, I cleared her heart chakra. She also had emotions trapped in her stomach area, due to childhood insecurity with her alcoholic father. I reassured her as I made my sounds.

Soon, Alice said, "I feel the energy leaving from my heart, and I feel less anxious."

We ended the session with her feeling better, and she wanted me to help her dog, Champ.

"What's Champ doing?"

"He helps keep the farm in order, as a herding dog. Something has changed, though. Is he sick? He's slacked off lately, sometimes disappearing into the nearby forest. He rarely did that before. This is different. It is happening more and more. Can you tell what is happening? We need him. He has a job!"

Champ was in the room with her. I asked him what was going on. He indicated he was fine, but a neighbor was letting his dogs go wild, and Champ was bringing food to them. Alice was surprised. Furthermore, I learned from Champ that he had made one of the dogs pregnant, and it gave birth to pups. I told him he had to tell Alice where these puppies were, so she could help with their care. I learned from Champ there were three of them, and I told Alice that.

As we were finishing her session, Alice said, "I'm shocked! My dog was not fixed; we were told not to do it. Those puppies will need care; it gets very cold here. Also, I will need another session with you."

A second session was held with Alice and with her daughter, who had epilepsy, and it was revealed that it turned out that Champ did have a canine partner, with three puppies, and he had been bringing food to them. Alice was amazed by the accuracy of my vision. Alice planned to adopt one or two of the pups. Also, her hair had stopped falling out and had gotten thicker, which she attributed to my mp3 broadcast on hair care that she had listened to repeatedly.

Animals have consciences, it seems. I was impressed by Champ's fidelity to his puppies and to their mother.

Alice's daughter's epilepsy we were able to reduce in intensity when I worked with grounding and clearing her energy. Elizabeth needed this, and said she felt clearer and less dizzy at the end of the session, and she was impressed with the speed of the improvement.

I have worked with owners and their animals for years. Champ's devotion to his puppies and their mother touched me. This was taking responsibility! I was glad to learn about it from Alice. The weather was turning cold, with winter coming on, and the pups might not have survived without the help from Champ and then from Alice. What a happy ending!

Chapter 14

Boo-Boo Zoo

A LADY WITH multiple sclerosis (MS), Sally, and her husband, Roger, wanted my help. They have a farm in Hawaii, the Boo-Boo Zoo for injured animals, an animal refuge.

Sally's illness made it harder and harder for her to walk, and it finally forced her to use a wheelchair. Meanwhile, she accumulated injured animals, and she found caring for them made her feel better.

It was years ago, and I would visit people on the Islands to help them. Somehow, Sallie heard about me. She showed up at the yoga studio, where I would work with people (and split the fees with the owner of the studio). I was there for about four years.

Sally had pain, real trouble walking. She hoped I could help. She was finding some solace being with her animals, but she was having some difficulty taking care of them, even though it was very good therapy for her.

Sally felt "lost," not knowing what she should do with her life. She was depressed for a while. Taking in the animals helped her feel better. She and her husband had about an acre of farmland for their menagerie, a variety of animals, almost like Noah and his ark.

In the first session, I tried to ease her pain and energize her. Her hands were swollen. She had trouble walking, too, and she feared a loss of mobility.

Meanwhile, the Boo-Boo Zoo was becoming popular. It required a lot of work, however, and Sally came to visit me to get help. She felt better after our sessions. I eased her pain, drug-free. We did not get a cure, but we did get some improvement. Her MS was too far gone for us to make a big change. We just made her more comfortable.

By the second session, she had acquired more animals.

By the third, she could not walk, and her husband was overwhelmed caring for the animals. It was just too much, though it was beneficial for her. The animals got along amazingly well, and some would even sleep in her bed.

I told her she needed more help, and in our session, we worked to get more abundance for her, to help her husband and her handle this.

In the third session, we worked on her body for the last time. She told me the good news that more people were coming to volunteer at the shelter. They also donated money, and the Boo-Boo Zoo had started to take off, even becoming therapeutic for the volunteers, as well as for Sally. Often the helpers were people who had been abused when young. Loving the animals helped them love themselves and each other. The love went all ways.

I have not heard from Sally in many years, as I now do my work on the phone, by Skype. I've learned that Sally has stabilized, and while her health is about the same, her spirits are high, and the animals deserve much credit for her continuing to enjoy her life despite the serious disability.

The moral of the story is that animals, of various species, somehow got along with each other at this second-chance zoo, and they helped the people who served get better themselves from their life traumas. The local newspaper has run stories about the impact Sally has had. There was an issue of a local magazine that carried many testimonials for the Boo-Boo Zoo and its beneficial influence on the volunteers as well as on the animals.

Chapter 15

───◆◆◆───

A PETTING ZOO, TOO

I RECENTLY RAN into a friend who works at the Maui Animal Farm...Heidi, now the owner. She remembered me from our earlier work. She has a petting zoo, for discarded pets, though they are not injured ones like those at the Boo-Boo Zoo.

I remembered her petting zoo; I would go to help the animals with my sounds, which seemed to calm them.

She invited me to return soon for a visit; they have few funds, and they rely on donations and volunteers. I give my work for free.

I had worked with a pony and calmed it.

The newly arrived animals sometimes find it hard to get used to their unfamiliar surroundings. I remember a goat that needed help. The poor thing was just a few years old, definitely showing unbalanced/blocked energy. This might have been due to a birth defect. I was told that its brain had needed more oxygen during delivery.

Heidi recalled this. She spoke of the help I gave a small pony, one that had lost its mother too early, lacked bonding, was nervous, needed calming. Often this is the most I can do with the animals, to reassure and ground them. Premature separation from the animal's parents is all too frequent.

Heidi was pleased to announce she had become the owner of the zoo, and she invited me back to help the flock. For example, she said, she had a pig, actually a smart animal, who could use some work.

The petting zoo gives tours and gets donations and volunteers. Heidi liked this much more than her former corporate job, and she found the work to be healing for her. It has become her passion.

People who come to Maui would like this, and they should donate to it or volunteer, as well.

I enjoy it. I hope to return there soon. I do love animals!

Chapter 16

FARMERS AND FOSTERS

SHELLY AND HER husband, Bart, needed help.

They have a farm that they have foster children help with, giving the kids a chance to be successful. This has helped many needy kids. The children work with the animals and get an improved sense of responsibility. They get paid a bit, too, for helping out. Often the kids get emotionally close to the animals.

Shelly had found me through a telesummit, wanting help with her chronic fatigue and sleep problems. Unlimited Energy was the program for her.

We did a session:

She is 67, living on a many-acre place in Texas. She has some help. She has had the fatigue issue for many years, getting older. Her kids became city kids, moving away to coastal cities. She has chickens, cows, and goats. Shelly and Bart sell dairy products, which has paid for much of their family expenses. Both she and her husband have found farming fun, but it is getting more challenging.

She has a women's group she socializes with, and that helps her. Her women's group has grown and has recognized her work.

She works with foster kids, to show them another life, one free of abuse, one with positive responsibilities, helping her and her husband, assisting with the animals, and cooperating with the other foster kids.

These children have changed Shelly's life, some returning just to thank her for getting them off drugs.

She has a summer program they run also: work-study, teaching responsibility. They teach the kids self-esteem, self-love, and the kids share their love with the animals, and often end up adopting pets for themselves. She told me how one teenager returned, having gotten a good job, a big contrast from living with his druggy family; he thanked her and told her he was going to college due to the farm program, and he has joined a youth group at the church.

Still, she deals with anxiety and low energy.

We began our session:

I told her, "Now, we need to work on you. First, we have to figure out why you have this energy problem. How were you raised?"

"I grew up on a farm, and we had what we needed, but our parents were distant emotionally. I now have taken on more responsibility than I want, having stretched myself too far. I lack enough help."

"Let's help your inner child to feel it is loved. We will clear your heart chakra and do a heart activation to teach your inner child self-love. We will move energy from within to a light above your head. We will clear some toxic belief systems, including the belief you have to do everything yourself." I made my sounds and moved her energy, and I released bonds from her past.

Soon after the session began, I told her, "Breathe more deeply. How are you feeling?"

It was only ten minutes into the session, and she reported she was feeling more loved and relaxed, two of the goals for my work with her.

Her inner child needed more loving. I worked on that.

"How are you feeling now?"

"Oh, my God, I am crying. Tears of joy. A surge of love. Your sounds are beautiful. You have a gift!"

"Take some more deep breaths. How are you feeling now?"

"So much better. I am feeling blessed!"

I recommended some meditations for her to do daily, and I showed her how to set up boundaries to keep her energy from being drained. She thanked me.

The success of the sound-therapy session pleased us both.

What is wonderful in this case, and is generally true, is that exposing children to animals helps the kids learn to share love, so both sides gain. Having a pet, having a farm, really helps people become more loving and be more responsible. People see such examples and often decide to get pets themselves.

Love is best when shared, and it echoes back and forth between the children and the animals they connect with. It is a shame that some people abandon these pets, hurting themselves and these animals by so doing.

Chapter 17

———◦∞◦———

MAUI ANGEL SAVES
DEATH ROW DOGS

WHEN I FIRST came to beautiful Maui, I worked at some oddball jobs. Some were with vendors at a mall, a mall with kiosks. One job was next to a toe-ring seller. (People pay thousands of dollars for such rings!) I chatted with the salespeople, especially with Emily.

As an animal lover, I gravitate toward similar people. Emily worked for the island's humane society awhile, but she could not make enough money to pay her expenses. She went into selling toe rings at a kiosk as a commissioned salesperson.

On Maui, you do what you have to, to live in Paradise.

Emily and I chatted about her love for animals, and some patrons would bring the topic up, too. Many new arrivals found the

Hawaiian animal quarantining rules to be oppressive. Hard to bring your pet here. No rabies allowed on Maui!

I remember waiting half a year to get my dog to the island from the mainland. We miss our pets.

Even though no longer working for them, Emily would still visit the humane society. There you could even pick up a dog for an outing, and the society would give you food to take with you, hoping that while on the trip, someone would get interested in adopting the dog. Now and then, that would happen, and a dog would find a home rather than have to be destroyed.

Emily worked in a busy tourist area, and lots of people would ask about the dog she was walking. They would ask about these "death row" dogs, and Emily would get them interested. People would often volunteer to take them home.

I remember "Peanut," a tiny Pomeranian-Chihuahua mix.

Unfortunately, people on the Islands seem to abandon their dogs if they have to move. Peanut had been in three different homes. Sweet little dog, and even I was tempted to adopt him. Emily took Peanut for one of her exhibition walks.

The next day, Emily said some people were crying over him; one woman was very sad he would die, but she could not adopt another dog, Then a guy told me that someone adopted him that morning, working people who wanted a small, lovable dog like Peanut.

Emily told me of several dogs who got adopted this way, shortly before they were going to be euthanized, put to sleep, killed.

PET TALK MADE CRYSTAL CLEAR!

Emily was passionate about this. She was an expert at placing doomed dogs in desirable domiciles.

I remember another mixed-breed dog, Chester, a Beagle mix, twelve years old, too old for most people to adopt. Again, Emily took him on a walk through the tourist area, and two days later, people came back to adopt Chester, having seen him on the Emily exhibition. He was adorable. Looked like a Dalmation-Beagle mix, floppy ears and spots.

Emily not only placed dogs, but she also sold more toe rings to people who were drawn in by the dogs. Sometimes the humane society would get calls from the people who had seen the Emily-exhibited dogs. For Chester they had so many calls, the society had to tell them, "first come, first served." Chester was full of life, and the people who adopted him were delighted, even though they had not originally intended to adopt a dog.

Emily was an angel in disguise. Her sweet "exhibitions" brought blessings to these dear dogs, and her kiosk was a financial success, almost as though the universe rewarded her for her good works. "What goes around, comes around."

Chapter 18

———❧———

KITTENS BORN IN THE BUSHES, NO ROOM IN THE INN

I WORKED FOR a major hotel for years. The job put food on my table, and I liked the people and the work. This chain employed me as a greeter with a kiosk on the oceanfront, giving our inn's welcome packets, along with coffee and information about local activities. I used to set up tours to display the hotel property. For about five years, I worked there, and I loved it, despite the high sales quota demands. A large, lovely property it was.

From time to time, a big, female, calico cat would come by, a hungry tabby cat. She'd show up out of nowhere. She'd lunch on lizards by the hotel's bushes. One evening, when not much was going on, I was at my kiosk, people-watching. The cat came again and then returned regularly for several weeks. I saw that she often stopped by a hedge near an unusual tree, and I found that she had kittens there! She was nursing four orange cats. I got some fish from the cafeteria and some water for her and the kittens.

A week or two after that, the kittens were out of their shelter, wandering around outside the hotel, where the management was eager to have them trapped to send to a shelter. A guest took a towel and grabbed one, naming him "Casper," then returned him to the kitten caboodle. One kitten, sadly, was lost.

A pool guy named them "PJ," "Tiger," and "Casper." They were similar but individual. Trapping had not worked at first, but later we caught them and had them neutered and given shots. The Maui Humane Society had no room for them, and cats don't need shelter on tropical Hawaii.

Some good Samaritan brought the cats back to the hotel, and we workers began hiding them, and some of the guests were playing with them. They became a feature, rather than a flaw, of the hotel. Guests would bring them snacks, and so did we.

Casper became our kiosk cart cat.

Tiger joined another kiosk.

We fed them both whenever they asked.

PJ was a pool cat, not a polecat, and Tom took care of him.

In effect, we hotel workers had been adopted by the foxy felines. The Humane Society would not take them, because they were "fixed" already, signified by a little notch cut in their ears. The Society leaves them in their environment, as there is nowhere to put them, and they are not causing trouble. And it's marvelous

Maui, for crying out loud...the house prices and the rents are sky-high and everyone and his cat want to live here.

Thankfully, one of the hotel's security guards accepted my explanation of why the cats should not be pestered.

They got bigger and even prettier, and friendlier. Casper especially made plenty of pals. He was a charmer. We made for him a "cat cabana" by draping a towel over a chair, and we added a sign to that effect, "Casper's Cat Cabana."

One Casper-loving guest made a Facebook page for Casper, and it still is on the 'net. Furthermore, Casper was not just a mouser, he was also a ratter, and he kept the rodents under control.

Casper had become a kiosk attraction, the owners acknowledged. He more than paid his way.

So, animals help us in many ways, including the cats who are keeping down the rodents and keeping up the spirits of those of us they entertain.

Chapter 19

———— ✤ ————

PURE PET PROVISIONS PRODUCER

SOMETIMES, YOU JUST know there is something wrong with your pet.

About a year ago, I worked with a woman who was starting a company to provide especially nutritious foods and supplements for people's pets.

She and her family have a farm, and they were able to control the production methods and produce wholesome pet provisions without pesticides.

Evelyn had found me through a telesummit. She has a nerve-damage disorder. The farm she has is in Ohio, owned with her husband; they were in their fifties, with three children, two boys and a girl. The farm had horses and goats and cows and chickens, along with a major vegetable garden.

She had found me on a telesummit, on which I was helping my callers get out of pain, help she needed, too.

We "met" on the phone, and I thanked her for signing up.

"Dawn, I'm just opening up to natural healing. I have had pain for many years. I have tried lots of doctors and various natural supplements. I reacted to one of those medications, and I am now cutting back on them. I'm willing to give your methods a try. Our daughter, Casey, 17, is helping to develop a line of completely natural products for people and pets.

I connected with Evelyn, doing my vocal sounds therapy. Her energy was clammed up, jammed uptight, which could have explained her pain. She was a worrier. I was very cautious in treating her anxiety, as she was very sensitive. I could see her injured inner-child.

I helped her release her pent-up energy, and this reduced her tension, helping her relax, as we tried to move her emotions from child to adult status. We wanted to update her thoughts.

"How are you doing now, Evelyn?"

"Good, this 25-minute session is definitely releasing my tension. I am going to have my daughter do this, too. Can you help pets? We have some limping goats that are our pets."

"Put them by the phone." I did some sound work within their hearing.

At the end of the session, she said she was doing better. She booked another session, this one for her daughter.

The session I had with her daughter was substantial, and we also did their pets. It was clear to me that Casey had absorbed the tension from her mom. She agreed.

I told her, "You are an unusually empathic teenager."

"Yes, sometimes, I feel I can hear people silently talking, reading their minds. This is so weird that I am afraid to leave the house at times."

"Casey, we will clear some energy that you have absorbed from your mom and others whom you know."

Toward the end of our session, she volunteered, "I am feeling much more peaceful."

"You need to establish healthy boundaries," I explained.

"Yes, it is hard for me to concentrate."

I showed her some "home-work" she could do to help herself. She should be able to have a social life.

"I feel a lot better, now."

We also had time to work on their goats, Pepper and Pastrami; both had tight hips. Casey told me the animals were listening, and something seemed to be happening, with one of the goats moving its legs in response to my sounds.

Next to be treated was Gilda, their Arabian horse, an older horse, one no longer used in their shows. She also needed healing of her arthritic legs. Casey and her mother thought they could see some improvement; they said the horse appeared to be curious and maybe even enjoying the sounds.

They later told me that Evelyn was feeling better, and they became convinced to specialize in wholly natural foods and supplements. They were going to make connections with stores like Whole Foods.

One of their products I later found at a feed supply store in Maui, within a year of our interactions.

So, these clients and their animals came to adopt a new way of living on their farm, now pesticide-free.

A recent (2020) review of pet foods was written by Erin Raub, and is available at this internet address: petlifetoday.com. She introduced her study as follows:

"As pet parents, you probably spend a lot of time thinking about the food your dog eats: What are the best organic dog foods? Which brands offer the best nutrition? What flavors does your pup like the best? Which foods offer the best cost-value balance? Options range from natural dog foods to organic pet food delivery services; then there are grain-free options, wholesome and holistic offerings, and high-protein dog foods – both as dried kibble and canned wet food – there are plenty of options for you to evaluate. Finding the right natural or organic dog food for your pet means reading reviews, studying ingredients lists, and diving into the ins and outs of natural vs. grain-free vs. organic dog foods.

"We reviewed dozens of organic and natural dog food brands

to find the best of the best, based on Amazon reviews, quality of ingredients, cost, and other considerations. We narrowed our search down to 5 of the top-rated natural and organic dog foods pet parents can purchase to ensure a healthy diet for their dog." You should go to the site for detailed information on what they found.

Chapter 20

RECENT INTERVIEWS

I HAVE ENJOYED being interviewed for radio and television programs. In early 2020, I had two that related to the subject of pets.

On February 14, 2020, I was interviewed on the internet radio program, "The Flea Circus." This is the link:

https://www.youtube.com/watch?v=l4QgUYypT6g&feature=youtu.be

The interviewers viewed favorably holistic methods, natural methods.

They liked that I was calling in from Hawaii. They noted I am a communicator with animals, one who can help with chronic illnesses, without medicine.

Chris Green was the principal interviewer, from KTTR radio of

Rolla, Missouri. The show is described as, "Each week [we] have a guest from the pet industry sharing insight into our furry friends. The host Chris Green has been hosting a pet Podcast called 'The Groomer Next Door' for 5+ years."

They asked how I went from living in the Midwest to settling in Hawaii. I told my story of early unhappiness, followed by eventual freedom. I was an outcast, one of six kids on welfare. "Searching for love in all the wrong places," had two failed marriages, held some interesting jobs, achieved some business success, but came near suicide, so I went to Hawaii to get a big change, 24 years ago. On the beach, I found my voice, and my vocalizations, by working on my own trauma.

In Hawaii, I found how to help people relieve their pain. Later on, some asked me to help their pets. Animals have always been my best friends, giving me unconditional acceptance. Even distressed animals. They knew I would be kind. They have souls, as we do. They seem to talk to me, not exactly in words, but somehow in ideas. I believe they go to an Afterlife once they die.

I told the interviewer that my earliest friends were pets, empathetic even when people were not.

Now I work with medical practitioners, and I help people with their energy issues that are causing them problems. The gift seems divine.

People find me by word-of-mouth, although I have gotten some notice internationally, especially through the internet.

It has been said, "When the student is ready, the teacher will appear," and I find some people quite receptive to my vocal sounds therapy.

Owners come for their telephone sessions and sometimes ask me to help their pets, too, and the pets seem to accommodate the treatment.

Our pets are our partners in ways we sometimes fail to recognize. They become extensions of ourselves. They sometimes absorb our moods. They can take on more energy than they can handle, and they need my help. Many are small and cannot absorb that much energy.

We should let them know that we love them and that we are ok. They will follow our lead.

This was Valentine's Day, and we talked about love.

The interviewers were impressed with how many books I have written. They wanted to know: how did I start to write? I explained that I like to try new things. I wanted to share with those whom I won't reach by phone, wanted to tell them there are alternatives. I wrote about pain, fear, energy, and happiness. Since pets are my true loves, I have been pleased to write about them, from cats and dogs even to birds and turtles and horses....

I always wanted to write a book, talked about it, then ended up doing it! Five times, so far!

I offered the listeners a free mp3 recording from www.dawncrystalhealing.com.

Soon after this, internet interviewer Mary Jane Popp and I discussed my work. The link is https://www.youtube.com/watch?v=36yy3xu549k&t=41s

Holistic methods with animals: how do I do it? I started with humans but gradually moved out to helping their pets. They communicate with us variously, including by telepathy.

The owners would come to me for their problems, and then ask whether I could help their pets. I help owners with pain, anxiety, etc. They wanted their pets helped too. Over 25 years, I got more and more into helping their pets. Each side influenced the other, humans and their pets, forming an interspecies family.

On some level, I can tell what they want. You probably can tell when they are hungry and when they want to go out, but I can sense some more.

I am connected with my animals, especially my dog, Hoku. I have a quiet home, where Hoku knows that if I am on the phone doing a show, he is to keep quiet, and then he will get a treat. My little Pug has gotten a bit chubby from such treats because he is so cooperative!

Over the years, I realized many owners needed my help with their animals. I found I could incorporate the pet in the session with the owner, doing the owner, my client, first, helping with my sound energy. The sounds also reached the animals if they were in the room with us.

My sounds dislodge blockages in our bodies, and allow our energy, what the Chinese call "chi," to flow and not stagnate. Stagnation produces discomfort. Little issues can become big ones, affecting all our organs.

Our pets connect with us. For example, a dog often attaches to one of the people in the household, bonding more with that one than with the others. The pets want to help us, and if we have trouble, they are upset, too.

A client will transfer stress energy to the pet, without meaning to. This can cause a problem that may not be fatal but can be disturbing, for example draining the pet of its energy.

I know when my dog is not well because he will not be playing with his squeaky toys, lying around instead. We want to nip this in the bud, or the butt, by incorporating the pet in the sounds-therapy session, having it listen in on the call or at least observe the improvement of the owner during the session.

Do dogs get sad? Yes, absolutely. During one period, I had to clear myself of my difficult past, and my dog at that time was aware of what was happening; when I was down, he would be down, too. Lethargy is the easiest sign to spot: pep is gone.

Trust is a big issue, too. Our pets need to trust us, trust that we will not hurt them, trust that we love them.

Animals have inherited levels of energy. I had a mother dog who stopped nurturing her puppies. She needed my work, probably due to inheritance, as her environment seemed fine. I was able to help her and thus her pups.

Do dogs get anxious? Yes. Mary Popp told me of a puppy she had that had been ignored in his youth and who would become very insecure when Mary left home even briefly.

Mary had a dog that had real anxiety issues, was very tense, yet who became a show dog once losing its tension. I told her how crate training helps make them more secure, especially if one makes a little fuss before one leaves the home.

Because of the fireworks that day, the Fourth of July is a time they greatly need reassurance.

An unusual case I had was of a dog with a body that was shutting down. The owners were afraid for its life. I did what I do, and a week later they reported the pet was much better. He is still alive. The secret? I had detected and removed much energy blockage. I have had some seeming miracles, although we know that all living things have a limited lifespan.

How do I do my long-distance work? I go worldwide by using Skype.

Animals understand us, want to love us and to bond with us. They forgive us for so much. They are here to support us, if we will let them. When I was not as aware, I did not realize that my pet's reaction to someone was a good guide as to whether the person was going to be beneficial for me. Now I know that.

In a simple form of communication, Hoku gives a little bark when he wants to be boosted to the coach.

Mary and I discussed: do pets pass over to an Afterlife? I think they do. I think they have souls.

At the end of the interview, I invited people to get my free recordings at dawncrystalhealing.com.

I enjoyed the interview. It was a pleasure to chat with Mary Jane Popp on her show, "Popp Off."

Rainbow Bridge

Just this side of heaven is a place called Rainbow Bridge.

When an animal dies that has been especially close to someone here, that pet goes to Rainbow Bridge. There are meadows and hills for all of our special friends so they can run and play together. There is plenty of food, water, and sunshine, and our friends are warm and comfortable.

All the animals who had been ill and old are restored to health and vigor. Those who were hurt or maimed are made whole and strong again, just as we remember them in our dreams of days and times gone by. The animals are happy and content, except for one small thing; they each miss someone very special to them, who had to be left behind.

They all run and play together, but the day comes when one suddenly stops and looks into the distance. His bright eyes are intent. His eager body quivers. Suddenly he begins to run from the group, flying over the green grass, his legs carrying him faster and faster.

You have been spotted, and when you and your special friend finally meet, you cling together in joyous reunion, never to be parted again. The happy kisses rain upon your face; your hands again caress the beloved head, and you look once more into the trusting eyes of your pet, so long gone from your life but never absent from your heart.

Then you cross Rainbow Bridge together....

— Author unknown, no copyright, obtained from site https://drmartypets.com/rainbow-bridge-poem/

Testimonials

These testimonials have been received by Dawn from those she has helped. We have made only minor revisions, mostly for readability and privacy.

Aloha!

Dear Dawn and team,

I wanted to share my amazing news -- I have been listening to the Healthy Joints programme for a total of 20 days (about 3 days per session on average, but more for the hips and knees session).

Prior to that I had a damaged cartilage on my left hip, I was in near constant pain, couldn't walk much, even sit much, couldn't carry my little boy for any distance...

I was referred to a specialist, had an MIR scan and the doctor said there was no cure for that... yes, he can do surgery and it will provide relief but no cure. I was supposed to be stuck with it for life.

Now, 20 days after listening to your healing sessions, I am pain free! I still feel an echo of that pain if I exert myself, but I am not in pain any more! THANK YOU, DAWN!

I am looking forward to my session with you (due in about 2 weeks' time).

Everyone says your sessions are life-altering!

All my love to you,

L

～～～

Hello,

I want to THANK YOU for the "work" that you do... I loved my one on one with you and the two programs that I purchased are uplifting - always feel lighter, taller, open and freer when I listen... Peace and love your way...

K

～～～

Dawn,

Thank you for helping me release pains when you were on webinar on Tue, October 29th. I was miserable, not feeling well with having some physical conditions, and I was in bed when I was joining the webinar.

I am feeling much better and did restart a small exercise on the next day even 30 min walk, and I realized whose work is very helpful to me. I could not do exercise for about almost one year until I got help from you.

I just finished module 1 for Joint pain. I am greatly impressed.

Beautiful! I look forward to future programs you develop. Thank you so much, Dawn.

Blessings,

K

Hello Dawn (or Aloha)!

I just have to say I am really having some results that I believe are from your remote energy. The first 2 days (Monday and Tuesday) I was doing some detoxing - extra eliminations, very tired the afternoon of the first day, etc. Today, (Wednesday) I was energetic, enthusiastic, started back in on a long-term project that I had just stopped working on.

Rock on!!!

Love,

M

ps - I am part of the current Learning Strategies "Sound Healing Silent Clearing" group, as well as purchasing your Darius package. I also purchased your Eram Saeed package - so I will be getting a second round of 21 days of remote healing.

Wow - cant wait to see what life is like after that!! And, oh yeah, I signed on for a one-on-one with you later in February.

Last night's Sound Healing/Silent Clearing with Dawn Crystal was... still is, Wonderfull (not a typo).

It felt like every cell in my body, and my auric field, were vibrating, and this was later on, After the session.

I was left feeling Much Lighter and, no longer burdened by the deep sorrow and pain from a relationship with Someone who has since passed on.

I am also so Grateful for those feelings- energies were brought so completely to the forefront just prior to the start of the session.

Source and Dawn have once again transmuted sorrow and pain into Joy and Light.

Thank you for sponsoring Sound Healing/Silent Clearing.

With much gratitude,

P

~~~

Hi, Dawn,

I just want to thank you so much for your healing session during the Soul Shine 2019. I feel so blessed to come across your session. It just resonated with me so much (I see I have this desire to tell my story ;)).

My life has been full of trauma as well. Both emotional and physical. To the point that I have something right now that's called a limbic trauma loop. I have very difficult to relax. Thanks to your online sessions/events and replays I have been able to feel some relaxation since a long time.

I really wish to work with you, because I just know/feel you can help me (further). Financially I am not able to book a session right now, so I just keep listening to the free recordings now. Hopefully, I will be able to book a session sometime. Thanks again.

Kind regards,

M

I am responsible for my life, and I don't intend to create dependency with or to anyone. But it is ok for everyone to get help as necessary. Dawn is the one I would ask for help or buy a product when I need to boost my energy.

Only products from others working for me are entity clearing and ancestral karmas.

I didn't do energy work on my own, but also did start belief clearing again after few weeks break.

I appreciate if you have a class like learning strategy course you regularly offer biweekly for 6 months. I can afford to join the course or do wait for any discount sales sometimes you inform via your email newsletter.

Two products I bought from pure light especially stomach one. I keep playing it when I can play without tech destruction.

I wanted to express sincere gratitude to you, Dawn, who helped me tremendously and the results what I got from this week's webinar was just beyond words.

N

Dawn,

Your generosity of Spirit and Compassion touches and humbles and inspires me each time we've worked together. Thank you.

(And I'm still heartburn free, Woo-HOO!).

Love,

P

~~~

Hola Dawn,

It's been 2 yrs since my last healing session with you. You helped me and my dog Cleo, who was diagnosed with cancer in the liver. She transitioned on 1-11-2018/11 and my time with her was special after our session with you.

I am writing in regard to another special friend her name is Kita. She's 16.5 yrs and will be transitioning soon. She is resilient. strong and full of life. She's not ready to let go yet and I feel she may have some messages for me and the family.

We would love a 30min session for her to receive messages and some energy clearing for her to make her transition that much easier and full of love.

Please advise as to which package you have for pets.

Gracias, Dawn, looking forward to reconnecting with you.

D

~~~

Hi Dawn,

What a Joy! I no longer need to cringe or contract when some traumatic experience raises up within me! Now I Feel it and Release it into God's Light, Poof! Gone!

You had asked where I had bought our 10/30/19 session from. I believe it was from the Eram Saeed, From Heartache to Joy, show and the package was Organ Regeneration.

It was like I heard your voice in my head, "order Whatever you want to eat for dinner!". So, I did, I had Italian, and, there was absolutely No heartburn afterwards! YAY! Thank you!!

Love,

P

Hi Liz,

I'm writing to thank you and Dawn for the session I had last Monday at 7pm (BST). I am so grateful to Dawn for all she did for me. I am with her Learning Strategies group since the second series. She worked so hard for me and gave me such strength. I am so sorry for the hassle with skype and so grateful to you Liz for letting me call your cell phone. I honestly can't tell you both how much the session strengthened me. And it continues to do so. I am so looking forward to Sound Healing Series #5!

Thank you both so much. Wishing you both a lovely day!

O.

Hi Dawn,

I hope this finds all is well with you and your Pupp.

Just a quick update....

For the First Time, since the back injury occurred over 4 years ago, I can turn completely around to my right side! I really appreciate that you sent the Complete, "Get Out of Pain Forever" Package. Your Compassionate Response is so very much appreciated. I'd felt waves of relief move over me as I listened to the "Clearing Back Pain" module. The pain has improved tremendously.

And, Thanks So Much for sending along the Wealth Revolution "Personal Awakening" package. I have felt unwinding and releases as I've listened to the Beautiful Music.

I continue to shake my head in Wonder and Joy at the Blessings from all the different modules.

From my Heart to Yours, Thank You Dawn!

Hi Dawn,

I am in such deep gratitude to you and your amazing work.

I contacted you to work with my beloved dog and not only did he receive healing, I also got an amazing session with you! You are a truly divine being and for anyone that is looking for healing... Dawn is an incredible healer...

Lots of love and gratitude

N

I'm so happy and grateful to have met Dawn Crystal. I find her energy and joy contagious. I've worked with Dawn for 6 months and so much has cleared from my mind and body. She is a healing blessing to me.

Thank you, thank you, Dawn. I am so thrilled.

G

Hi Dawn,

My name is K****.

I heard you recently on Cari Murphy's podcast.

Thank you for following your Heart and Sharing your Gifts.

I look forward to signing up in the next few days via Cari's site.

I want to thank you for making the session with you so affordable.

It will allow so many to step in and feel the God Self with greater ease.

Many Blessings and A Love Pat to your Furry Friends.

You will hear from me soon.

Mahalo,

K

Hi Dawn, This is me, dancing with Joy. I had deliberately waited to get my Pupp's bloodwork repeated to give his Healing time to process. I Knew we would get Good News and we Did! His white blood cell count & lymphocytes are Normal! His blood platelet count went from 75,000/80,000 (low) to 305,000, gloriously Normal! It feels to me that our bond together has deepened as well.

My hip and lower back pain are Gone! I have now found an affordable Handyman that I believe will do a great job, allowing me to (finally!) put my home on the market. The fatigue persists, which makes me wonder what Lesson I have yet to learn or remember, or, what past Life issue may be raising up for healing. I may be making another appointment with you.

Your humbleness, clear Intent and Focus on Only that which is to the Highest, Greatest Good, and determination that no ego only Source is what is are Inspiring and humbling. I So Appreciate and am Grateful to you and Source. I hope your Pupp's leg is All Better! Congratulations on & many Blessings in your new Home!

From Zorro & my Hearts to Yours,

Thank you! Thank you! Thank you!

Love, B

I have sought out and have paid so many sound healers and nothing shifted for me.

Until I heard a radio show Dawn Crystal was doing. Something shifted for me by just listening to the replay of this radio show. Dawn Crystal is the real deal and definitely sent to us by the Divine. I booked a session, I was somewhat skeptical but my intuition said do it, loud and clear.

It was amazing. Dawn shared that the process would be working for a while after my session. It's been two weeks today and I have not felt this joyous and free in 20 years. Give yourself the best gift ever, work with Dawn Crystal, I will continue to work with her as long as she is doing this work.

Bless you Dawn. Your healing is a miracle.

M

Dear Crystal,

I am deeply grateful to you for the healing that you gave to me this past Saturday. While I have been working for the last 6 months on relationship issues in this lifetime and healing the many soul contracts I have had with my father, husbands and men in my life, as well as female authoritarians, I have only recently been touching on my own feminine issues and relationships with women.

I was aware that the sadness and loss of not being loved was still in me, and aware that not being loved was both a genetic line issue and a soul contract that I had made in for this lifetime, I was not aware of my issues related to my abortion nor was I aware that his soul was still present in my body. Didn't even know that was possible.

Following my healing, when I went to bed, my uterus started contracting as though I were giving birth. Given that I was sleep deprived from all the individual work I had done for the previous two weeks, I took a homeopathic remedy for muscle spasms and wounds. It immediately relaxed and I slept for 10 hours.

The next day, I woke up experiencing a lot of grief. A friend, who is psychic, came over and saw the soul and identified him as a loving, active boy. We had a discussion and she offered that I needed to welcome him back into my womb and release him to Creator. I did that three times.

This morning I lit a candle to honour him and send him on his way. I now feel at peace and ready to move on to the next issue that arose in my dreams.

I am deeply grateful to you for helping me take one more step on my road to healing wherever it leads me.

Blessings to you and your work,

S

I lost my back right third molar, more than ten years ago while eating corn nuts. I couldn't tell what tooth was and what was corn nut at the time. OMG. With Great hope I bought Dawn Crystal's Dental Care package. MY TOOTH GREW BACK!!!! It's once rough, jagged edges smooth now as a normal tooth should be! What Just Happened!?? THANK YOU Dawn!! You Are a Rock Star in sound healing m'dear!! TY TY!!!!

K

Dear Dawn,

"Miraculous" is the word that keeps coming to mind as every day brings the Joy of discovering something else that has been Transformed. And each return to Balance feels as natural as Breathing!

I feel like I have come back to Life, Lighter & more Present with myself.

A back injury... Healed! No more pain! I had listened to the Joint segment of Total Body Rejuvenation ONCE and my hips are remarkably better. I discovered this as my Pupp & I were hiking in the park & I Felt So Much more Comfortable!

I was brushing my teeth when I realized that the tooth pain was Gone! We had worked on "fear" for literally a few minutes and, the next time something "scary" had happened - I Felt Calm, and the phrase that popped into my head was, "I Am Strong!", and, I Felt that!

And the Messages you gave me from my Beautiful Daughter who had passed a month before our Private Session have Transformed my Life! Yes, there are times I cry, times I would like to text or call her, of course! But now, the predominant feeling is one of Joy, of Relief - She Really IS OK! More than "ok", she Is Filled with Joy & Peace & Love, & is having a Grand Adventure in her New Life! I "knew" that before, now, I Really Know it!

There's more too, but I think the above conveys that Dawn Crystal IS the Real Deal! What it may not convey is your Authenticity, your genuine Compassion, and the Nonjudgmental, Caring ways you interact with those of us Blessed with meeting you and being Transformed through your Gifts. I am So Grateful for the Wonderful Changes you have, and still are, through your recordings, bringing about in my Life.

Thank You Dawn Crystal. Many Blessings to You!

Love,

B

Dear Dawn Crystal,

Your sessions are a great help for me, a very positive transformation is going on!

I always believed in the healing capacities of sound, and now you give me the opportunity to discover by your beautiful and powerful voice the incredible benefits of it.

I am very grateful for this magnificent present I received from you!

Thank you so much!

You changed my life!

Love,

A

Hello Dawn,

Yes I would love to write you a testimonial!

I always feel at a loss for words just as the healing you do is beyond words. It is in the etheric and energetic realms that then transform into the physical. I feel more energy, liveliness, sparkle and joy in life.

K

Hi Dawn & or Dawn's team!

I'm a bit of an energetic being so I will do my best to put some of my experiences into words. You may need to pick out chunks for a testimonial. and I this is not at all coherent its ok to delete it!

I found Dawn through Learning Strategies. I was on the 1st series she did. I would have been on more, but somehow, I didn't know she did more than one. It was wonderful. I had hip pain when I slept, and the 1st time I listened while I was listening my hip pain went away. That blew me away! I listened to them intermittently and enjoyed it. It made a huge shift in my relationship with my husband. I used it to clear issues with my dog. I do a lot of other energy clearing stuff, so I got sidetracked. I was always curious but never ambitions enough to look up Dawn on the internet until about February. I was out on a bike trail with the dogs & slipped on ice & broke my leg. I had a lot of down time, so I looked her up. I was looking online for a private session. On like how did I create this how can I uncreate this what else is possible? And what can I clear so it doesn't happen in the future? That kinda looked like a dead-end street, but I signed up for her email.

So, with the Total Body Rejuvenation I kept listening to the Ankle one a lot. I do think it has helped the healing process. I have also listened to the teeth one & that has been great. I've unfortunately had a lot of dental work a & had to have 2 crowns this winter as well & it has been wonderful!

I got the new dental package as well & the coolest thing about that is that my teeth feel cleaner after I listen to it. I also had a tooth that had a fill that hurts & it hurts a lot less now. I still can't floss behind it, but I have started chewing on that side of my mouth.

I have no desire to get sick but if I do, I know I can out one of your mp3's on & clear it which is phenomenal!

Do you of have you considered doing something on sleep? My husband has problems sleeping.

Thank you for being you & in the world & on the planet (yes possibly the same thing). Thank you for being as weird & wonderful as you are and using your gifts & talents to contribute to the world.

And finally, I just have to say this is really weird. This is probably the longest email I've written ever.

Thank you

M

Dear Friends,

I participated on a free online course with Siegfried. I'm sorry I can't recall all her name, yet it was a gift indeed as she introduced Dawn amongst many guests.

Dawn was one of two who touched me very deeply in a short video where she used her 'sounding.'

This went so deep as if an invisible hand was reaching inside me and lifting out what was ripe to be released, in my case emotional pain.

Sound has always been a close friend of mine though strangely i can't listen to much music these days.

Dawn's sound expression though had a wholly new expression, very pure and liberating. I could feel her journey that she shared as this gift was given to her.

I would want everyone to be free from pain and know that Dawn will be able to assist humanity to a new place of freedom.

Thank you.

J

I always feel at a loss for words just as the healing you do is beyond words. It is in the etheric and energetic realms that then transform into the physical. I feel more energy, liveliness, sparkle and joy in life.

K

Dawn Crystal's Anti-Aging and Total Body Rejuvenation sound healing PDFs feel miraculous! A literal Godsend.

I only wish they could be used without headphones from a CD or cassette for less EMF radiation. (Cannot be used without WiFi/cellular connection.) Would use more often this way.

Thank you, Dawn Crystal, for sharing your spectacular gifts!

D

About The Author

Dawn Crystal, an internationally recognized Voice Sound Healer, Body-mind Intuitive, respected Intuitive Life Coach, Soul Reader, Medium, Pain Release Expert and Best-selling Author (*PAIN FREE Made Crystal Clear!, FEAR FREE Made Crystal Clear!, HAPPINESS Made Crystal Clear!, FATIGUE FREE Made Crystal Clear!*), is known as a **LEADING TRANSFORMATIONAL EXPERT** incorporating ancient wisdom for modern-day success.

Dawn is passionate about helping people clear emotional and physical blockages, so they can manifest from their higher selves, step into their full potential, and lead their lives and businesses in ways that align effectively with their souls' purpose.

Dawn helps her clients to release themselves quickly from pain, emotional and physical, and she is an active mentor for entrepreneurs, CEOs, and celebrities, helping everyone! Dawn is the "go-to" person to get out of pain fast, in minutes!

Dawn participates regularly on global teleseminars, radio shows and podcasts. Dawn was recently interviewed by the *Today Show, Dr. Oz, Rachel Ray, The View*, etc. Dawn hosts her own radio show, *Pain Free Fast & Easy!* on the News for the Soul Network. For the past two years she has done a live bi-weekly program at Learning Strategies Corporation of Minneapolis called, "Sound Healing / Silent Clearing."

Dawn's unique sound healing CD has been purchased by clients around the globe, and she is available on both phone and Skype, as well as for teleseminars.

Dawn lives a peaceful life on Maui, along with her adorable dog, Hoku.

Dawn has already published four books in this series,

PAIN FREE Made Crystal Clear

FEAR FREE Made Crystal Clear

HAPPINESS Made Crystal Clear

FATIGUE FREE Made Crystal Clear

all published by Outskirts Press, available in paperback and ebook formats from Outskirts and from Amazon (amazon.com) and Barnes & Noble (bn.com).

"I wouldn't change anything about my life; it's a gift," she affirms, and she transmits this inner strength to those she works with, giving them a grounding, a stable psychological place abounding with safety and love.

"I wouldn't do it over again, but I am glad where I ended up."

To see a ten-minute interview video with Dawn Crystal, go to https://tinyurl.com/ybg3osgp .

To see almost 100 videos featuring Dawn Crystal, go to https://www.youtube.com/channel/ UCTVOeWAA5eI0_5T4Eagcn7Q/videos

REVIEW *PET TALK?*

Reviews on sites such as amazon.com help connect readers and authors. We would appreciate it if you would write a review, even a short one.